Am I Enough?

FROM A SHACK TO A CASTLE
FOR THE KINGDOM

BY JENNIFER WATLINGTON

All Scripture quoted is from the New International Version of the Bible, unless otherwise noted.

For my mom,

Your faithful love and prayers and your selfless heart
have been a constant source of strength in
my life-always interceding to the Father on my behalf.

My precious husband Alex,

Your love for Christ brought me to you,
and it is written on every page of my life story.

And my daughters,

Sarah, Abby, and Makenzie

You inspire me daily to be brave and to never stop
chasing after Christ. I love you all with all of my heart.

TABLE OF CONTENTS

Isaiah 61:1-3

"The Spirit of the Sovereign Lord is on me,
because the Lord has anointed me
to proclaim good news to the poor.
He has sent me to bind up the brokenhearted,
to proclaim freedom for the captives
and release from darkness for the prisoners,
to proclaim the year of the Lord's favor
and the day of vengeance of our God,
to comfort all who mourn,
and provide for those who grieve in Zion—
to bestow on them a crown of beauty
instead of ashes,
the oil of joy
instead of mourning,
and a garment of praise
instead of a spirit of despair.
They will be called oaks of righteousness,
a planting of the Lord
for the display of his splendor."

Introduction

If you are reading these words, then I have already prayed for you. God, in His infinite wisdom and sovereignty, has brought you to the place you are in at this very moment. Dear friend, during our time together, I pray that you get a glimpse of the beauty and joy that God desires for you. You are His beloved child and He wants to take all of your anxiety, fear, heartache, and shame in exchange for all that is good and loving. God is not angry or disappointed in you. Psalm 139:17 says, "How precious to me are your thoughts, God! How vast is the sum of them! Were I to count them, they would outnumber the grains of sand —when I awake, I am still with you." Can you imagine being thought about millions and millions of times by our loving and merciful God? That is exactly what scripture is saying about His thoughts toward you.

Unfortunately, we live in a broken and fallen world where sin is prevalent and far-reaching. Satan invades the lives of those willing to carry out his mission who are unaware of the truth of the Gospel. Satan uses them to wreak havoc in the lives of God's children. The Word says in John 10:10, "The thief comes only to steal and kill and destroy . . ." Satan cleverly and strategically manipulates unknowing vessels to carry out his deceptive plans to destroy the lives of countless men and women. There are consequences to the destruction he brings, and often sin is passed from generation to generation. His aim is to wound and defeat the children of God so that you and I would be blind to the truth of God's Word. I want to share with you that no matter what you have experienced, whether by the actions of others or even by your own doing, God loves you today, yesterday, and forever. There isn't anything you can do that changes His love for you. He desires for you to know His unconditional, all-encompassing, unrelenting, unwavering, perfect love of God in every part of your being. Precious friend, no matter where you are in this moment, open your heart and begin to imagine a life where you don't have to worry, or strive, or earn acceptance and value. I know this may sound too good to be true, but I assure you, it is not! And trust me, I understand what it is like to feel unworthy and undeserving of God's blessing. I know the shame and pain of feeling like I would never measure up or be good enough to earn the love of others; much less the love of Almighty God.

When I was a child, I loved reading wonderful fairy tales where the impoverished young girl is swept away by the kind, handsome prince. She becomes his princess and they live happily ever after. As the Lord began healing my wounded soul several years ago, I found myself drawn to Isaiah 61. He showed me the truth of His Word, and as I gained understanding, a story began to unfold in my heart. I want to share it with you here, and I pray that as you read it, the Holy Spirit will take your imagination to the tiny, little broken-down shack; a place where so many of God's children still live today. May you begin to see yourself as God sees you; in the light of Christ. This is the story of an ordinary girl who grew up in the shadow of shame and disappointment. Let's call it…

"A Tale of an Unlikely Princess"

Once upon a time in 'The Land of Not So Far Away' lived a young peasant girl named Jenni. The little girl and her parents lived in a tiny, broken-down shack right in the middle of the richest kingdom in all the world. The kingdom's vast landscape was magnificently arranged. Soaring high above the rooftops were beautiful, strong oak trees adorned with thick, velvety leaves. At the base of the trees were brilliant shades of green foliage extending as far as the eye could see. Every inch of the kingdom was covered in this heavy green blanket, except for the very spot on which the little shack stood. The ground surrounding the hovel was barren with not so much as a tree, bush, or even a single blade of grass. It appeared as nothing more than an inconvenient eyesore, but to the little girl and her family, it was the only home they had ever known.

The family tried to enjoy each other and the life they shared in the little shack. They would play games, sing songs, and tell stories in order to pass the long, cold, dark nights. It was a way to forget the nagging feelings of fear and dread that would certainly haunt them tomorrow, just as it had in days past. For the kingdom had a charming and cunning king who had been the ruler of 'Not So Far Away' longer than anyone could remember. King Cruel controlled everyone in the kingdom and had a heart as hard as his angry fist. The King was deceptive and practiced his deception with a smile on his face. He had a special hatred for the family living in the shack. He had heard that the little girl's father had a special plan for her life, and this outraged the king. His desire to be in complete control made him more determined than ever to make life in the shack as dark and oppressive as possible.

In this kingdom, there were certain tasks performed only by the lowest of the low. Cleaning the ashes from below the stovepipes was looked upon as a task that no upstanding, self-respecting person would ever do. To gain favor with the people, the king decided that this task was too terrible for ordinary people to perform. So naturally, King Cruel made a decree that this would be, for all times, the duty of the young, peasant girl, Jenni.

To ensure that the family would not forget their lowly position, the king forced them to heap the enormous piles of ashes outside the windows of the broken-down shack. The filthy, black piles towered high above the roof of the shack, casting a dark shadow onto everything beneath it. The shadow of the ashes covered every window and crack in the wall, blocking all light. The darkness was an attempt to imprison the family and tighten the grasp of the evil king.

One can only imagine how difficult life must have been for the family. Their attempts at happiness were constantly challenged by adversity and hard times.

Evil forebodings and fear of the king became part of their daily lives. Despite their oppression, the young daughter fought desperately to lighten the hearts of her family. Young Jenni realized that her kind words and pleasing smile brought a bit of joy to her parent's sadness. As time passed, her smile seemed to become frozen across her face. She hid her true feelings from everyone behind her icy wall.

It was only late into the night, when the little shack was still and quiet that Jenni would allow herself to mourn for her family's situation. She used her finger to write secret prayers to God on the wall. She knew little about God, for King Cruel banned all Scripture many years before. She did, however, sense God's presence and hoped He would one day come to her rescue.

After many years, a miraculous event occurred in the kingdom. A grand celebration was planned by order of King Cruel where he would set sail in a high flying, hot air balloon. He boasted that he would be the first in 'The Land of Not So Far Away' to ever attempt such a feat. Despite severe storm warnings provided to him by local officials, King Cruel insisted on carrying out his plan. No one would dare oppose the king, so he set sail in the hot air contraption just as the clouds began to grow dark.

As expected, the storm seized upon the kingdom with a fierce and mighty wind. The wind whistled through the tunnels and down the winding streets, carrying with it anything and everything not firmly secured to the ground. Unfortunately for the king, his balloon was caught up in the gale and was carried off into the distance with the king never to be seen or heard from again.

After the storm clouds passed, the people of the kingdom began to emerge with a sigh of relief. Although no one wished harm upon the king, his presence most certainly would not be missed.

For Jenni, there was an even greater miracle that occurred that day. The towering piles of ashes surrounding the little shack had disappeared! Although it took years of toil and heartache for the shadowy piles to grow, the ashes were gone in an instant, thanks to the almighty wind. Jenni could barely open her eyes as she was struck by a magnificent ray of sunshine coming through the window. She had never seen such light inside the little shack. It was as if the great cloud of darkness lifted and a bright light of hope began to shine. Jenni's secret cries to God had not only been seen and heard, but they had been answered in a way that far exceeded her wildest dreams.

The years passed, and Jenni grew into a young woman. She met and fell in love with a kind, handsome prince. They were married and she became his princess. She was loved by her prince and treated well by all that knew her. She was blessed with three precious daughters. Her new home was a beautiful castle overlooking an enchanted kingdom. She dressed in the finest clothes in all the land.

Odd as it may seem, the princess did not feel any different than she had as a young peasant girl growing up in the shack. When she glanced into the mirror, she did not see the fine linens she was wearing but rather her old, tattered clothes of despair. When she gazed out the window at the magnificent grounds surrounding the palace, she only saw the pitiful, broken shack covered with the shadowy, black ash piles. She couldn't even express her struggles, for she still wore her frozen smile from her past. Though Jenni had received a new life, she still needed the most important thing – a new heart.

The prince sensed her sadness. Unlike the princess, he had grown up in a land where love, peace, and joy were constant companions. God's word was read frequently, and God's name was exalted throughout his life. He loved his princess and began to pray for her day and night.

One evening, the princess laid on her bed alone. It had been many years since she had written her secret writings on the wall. Although she was removed from the darkness of her past, memories of that time continued to haunt her. She remained resentful of the king and carried a burden of shame and unforgiveness that became too much to bear. At that very moment, her dear prince placed a book beside her. She opened the book and began to read. Instantly, a beautiful Spirit descended before her. The Spirit opened His hand which contained an exquisite bottle. The bottle contained the oil of gladness with the power of true, unconditional love. He shared with her the truth of salvation and of Jesus' sacrifice.

Princess Jenni knew deep inside her heart that she was dearly loved. It no longer mattered if she lived as a peasant in a broken-down shack or as a princess in the most magnificent castle in all the land. She was worthy of His love simply because of the free and perfect gift of salvation. She realized that God had always loved her; even when the dirty ashes were all she could see. She felt the weight of her own sin of unforgiveness and understood clearly the need to be forgiven, as well as the power to forgive. For the very first time, she saw herself in the light of Christ. The light of salvation was all she needed to finally escape the darkness.

Princess Jenni fell to her knees; her head bowed with her hands raised to the sky. She began thanking the Father for His Son and for His amazing love. She experienced complete healing for all the years of fear and sadness that had imprisoned her for so long. She began to weep for the first time in many, many years. Her frozen smile melted away by her own tears cascading down the sides of her cheeks. It was replaced by a soft, gentle grin that filled her face with light.

As she rose to her feet, she was amazed at the transformation her Father had made. Her sadness and mourning had been replaced with the oil of gladness. She looked into the mirror and to her amazement, she no longer saw her tattered clothes of despair, but she saw a beautiful garment of praise. As she looked out the window, she was struck by the site of the tiny, broken-down shack. The oppressive piles of ashes that had always towered above her had vanished. They were replaced with the most brightly colored flowers imaginable. The shack was surrounded by rich, green oak trees soaring into the clouds.

The Father had a plan and brought it to completion. The little girl that was once a lowly ash collector was now a joint heir to the throne of God. All of her old life had passed away and everything was made new. The Lord bestowed on her a crown of beauty instead of ashes, the oil of gladness instead of mourning, and a garment of praise instead of a spirit of despair.

According to those who still live in 'The Kingdom of Not So Far Away', the tiny, broken-down shack stands to this day. It remains among lovely colored flowers and alongside the soaring oaks of righteousness; a planting of the Lord. It serves as a reminder to all who know its story, as a display of the Father's splendor and glory.

Chapter 1

Jenni

Obviously, I am not a princess, and this is not my story. I did not grow up in 'The Land of Not So Far Away' under the control of King Cruel nor did I collect ashes from stovepipes. Actually, my story is quite different. I know Jenni well however, and I am all too familiar with her companions of dread, shame, and fear. Like her, I grew up in a very volatile home where evil was never very far away.

Early in my life, I learned the scripture Jeremiah 29:11, "For I know the plans I have for you," declares the Lord, "plans to prosper you and not to harm you, plans to give you hope and a future." There is great comfort in knowing that the Creator of the universe has a good plan for His children. Something that I have come to realize as I have grown in my walk with the Lord, is that Satan also has his agenda and plan for our lives.

While God's plan results in freedom through our obedience to Him and His Word, Satan's plan is for ruin and destruction through disobedience. Jenni, like me, was just an ordinary girl. She wasn't particularly pretty, and she didn't come from a wealthy family. It wasn't as if she were born into some affluent or distinguished life. That, however, did not matter to

Satan. His aim is to seek and destroy all that God intends. God loved Jenni, and Satan knew it. Satan set little Jenni and her family in his sights, and he was determined to use the king to carry out his plans for their destruction.

There were many events in my early life orchestrated by the enemy. By a decree of the king, I began gathering my ashes. One of my earliest memories was when I was in the second grade. I was the little girl with blonde hair, very pale skin, and blue eyes which were hidden behind thick, brown-rimmed glasses. I worked very hard to make good grades and I desperately wanted to please my teachers. My teacher nominated me for the 'Second Grade Sweetheart Pageant'. I remember being so excited to be in a pageant. I later learned that the winner was chosen by the teachers, but for that one night, I felt special. My mom went to the local department store and purchased my outfit for the pageant. I am sure the purchase was a sacrifice, but as always, she worked hard and strived to give me her very best.

The dress was a blue, polyester business suit with a pleated skirt. I wore white knee socks and black, patent leather 'Mary Jane' shoes. I can remember looking in the mirror and thinking that I looked like a grown-up. When we arrived at the school and began to line up backstage, I was greeted by all of the other little girls. They were all wearing short, ruffled, lace dresses with fancy little rolled down socks and white shoes. They had big bows in their hair and none of them were wearing glasses. Even as a seven-year-old girl, Satan began whispering untruths in my ears.

To my surprise, I won the pageant that night. I could not believe it! I will never forget the red sash that was put over my shoulder. I remember feeling so special. The next day I walked into my classroom expecting to be greeted with hugs and cheers, but instead, I was approached by several of the other girls in the class. They told me that their grandmothers could not believe I won because I was the ugliest girl in the pageant. Those words still ring in my ears 40 years later. How cruel to mock and taunt a child? Satan knew my family situation, and he took full advantage of my vulnerabilities. He began his siege upon my young heart, and he did not relent until I began to recognize God's voice among the shadows.

Chapter 2

The Evil King

God is perfect and holy, and He intends His very best for His children. Before the fall of Adam and Eve in the garden, they enjoyed close fellowship with Almighty God. They had no worries or fear – only peace and joy with God. This was God's original plan.

Satan, however, also has a plan. In Ezekiel 28:12-19, we are given a realistic picture of who Satan was before he was cast from heaven, "You were the seal of perfection, full of wisdom and perfect in beauty . . . You were anointed as a guardian cherub, . . . till wickedness was found in you." Before the foundation of the world, Satan was created to be a wise, beautiful, powerful, and 'anointed' cherub. He was considered blameless, until unrighteousness was found in him. God treasured the beauty and power bestowed to Satan. As pride rose up in Satan's heart, he began to expect more and more. He was not thankful nor did he trust in the wisdom and sovereignty of God. He began to view God as an equal, and he became consumed with a desire to have all that God possessed. Because of his pride and envy, he was cast from heaven and thrown into the pit. Satan became the enemy of God, and his rebellion towards God continues to provide fuel for his assault on mankind.

Satan plants seeds of pride into the minds of unsuspecting men and women, and He is always clever in his deception. He doesn't present prideful thoughts with clearly marked signs of danger. The thoughts are disguised under the precepts of the world's standards for success; be more, have more, do more. God never intended for us to be consumed with thoughts of self. Pride tells us that if God loves us, he will give us all we desire. Our view of God becomes distorted. As pride grows in our hearts, we wander down a path of working and striving to find happiness and fulfillment from a world that is unable to satisfy. Blinded people spend their entire lives chasing after an infinite promise of success and acceptance, only to find it to be a cruel, unattainable mirage.

In the garden of Eden, Satan disguised himself as a serpent and then spoke to Eve as if he were a trusted friend. He deceived Eve with a logical idea that God must be withholding his best from her. When Eve reminded Satan that eating the fruit would be an act of disobedience to God, Satan argued that eating the fruit would result in her being like God. He was so good, how could that possibly be wrong? It is ironic that Satan strategically tempted Eve with the same thought that resulted in his being cast from heaven. Satan knew the destructive power that arises from pride. It is from Eve's sin and Adam's, that our sinful natures arise. Satan works overtime to preoccupy our minds with thoughts of self-gratification and self-preservation; both of which prevent us from having a mind and heart focused on following the will of God.

Satan leads us to believe that if God is truly loving and kind, then he will prevent suffering and hardship and only allow good things for his children. This type of thinking led to Satan's downfall and if allowed to grow in our hearts, it will lead to our downfall as well. Behind every man and woman who live in rebellion against God, there is the Adversary, whispering little lies, always accusing, deceiving, and leading his victims down a path of wanting and deserving more; a path that is bound for destruction.

Proverbs 8:13 says, "To fear the Lord is to hate evil. I hate pride and arrogance, evil behavior and perverse speech." The sin of pride in Satan was the original sin which gave birth to all other forms of evil. We, as believers, are commanded to fear the Lord because fear and reverence toward the Lord produces humility. Humility stands in direct opposition to pride. Honoring the majesty and glory of God ensures a right heart attitude toward the Father and protects our minds against the enemy.

Satan works through anyone who is willing to engage in sin. He is the counterfeit to God. He is cunning and clever and masks himself as an angel of light. His goal is to bring destruction to as many lives as possible. In Jenni's story, King Cruel was being used by Satan to attempt to destroy God's plan for her life. He used fear and intimidation, along with shame, to remove all hope from her heart. The shadowy piles of ashes were his efforts to keep her from seeing the light of God and the truth of salvation. Satan knew that wounding Jenni's spirit and creating doubt in her very existence and purpose would keep her from seeing God's love for her. Satan was also planting seeds of pride in Jenni's heart. How could a loving God allow such hardship and pain in the life of a child that He supposedly loves? Surely, she deserved better from a loving God.

Job was a righteous man of whom God was well pleased. We read in Job chapter 1 that Satan approached God and asked about God's servant Job, "Does Job fear God for nothing?" Satan assumed that Job loved and worshiped God for what God could do for Job rather than for God Himself. Satan believed that if he brought affliction to Job, he would curse God and refuse to worship Him. That was his hope and his intent. Satan was unable to attain God's power while in heaven, so he tempted Job to curse God in an effort to exert his power on earth. Satan uses the same strategy with us today as he cleverly suggests that if God is loving and worthy of praise, then he must answer our request to have more and be better. We must guard against this way of thinking as these are the thoughts of the great Deceiver. Rather, we must praise God at all times and in all circumstances; this is a true heart of worship. Praising God through difficulty combats the lies of the enemy and provides spiritual armor for our hearts and minds.

Chapter 3

The King's Decrees

In Jenni's story, King Cruel made a decree that gathering the ashes from below the stovepipes would be the duty of the young, peasant girl forever. The King made certain his opposition to the plan her father had for her was known. He knew that the ashes would serve as a constant reminder of her shame. Through generational and familial sins, Satan continues to assign destructive behaviors to God's children. Without the knowledge of a loving and forgiving Father, sin is always accompanied by shame. A person motivated by shame is forced to hide their sin which prevents closeness and transparency in relationships both with people and with God. Just like a predator isolates its prey from the herd, Satan's plan is to separate his victims in order to suggest that his way is the only answer to the problem. He intends to create loneliness and darkness in a person's mind so that the light of Truth is hidden. Satan understands that like Jenni's ashes, shame creates isolating wounds that render a heart broken; a brokenness that can only be repaired by the One who created the heart.

In Scripture, Satan has several different titles including the Enemy, the Evil One, the Destroyer, the Tempter, the Prince of the World, the Father of Lies, the Great Deceiver, the Accuser, the Serpent, a

Roaring Lion, etc. Today, Satan continues to attack God's children, but he wears many different masks such as alcoholic, child abuser, abusive spouse, drug addict, human trafficker, eating disorders, worry, poverty, illness and disease, anxiety and depression. . . the list goes on and on. Many times, Satan seeks to use individuals that are victims of sin and abuse to carry out his plans. These people are wounded and easily deceived into believing his lies. Unless the truth of Christ casts light into the darkness of a person's heart, sin continues from generation to generation. Romans 12:2 speaks to the importance of renewing our minds in Christ. "Do not conform to the pattern of this world but be transformed by the renewing of your mind. Then you will be able to test and approve what God's will is – his good, pleasing, and perfect will." God's Word has the power to break away the ash-polluted lenses that Satan has cunningly placed upon our eyes.

Scripture reminds us that Satan roams around like a roaring lion seeking whom he may devour. He seeks out the vulnerable and attacks with subtle, destructive lies and accusations. He takes advantage of weaknesses, and he shows no mercy. Whether it is the loss of a loved one, a health ailment, financial difficulties, failure to accomplish goals, or rejection in a relationship; Satan distorts the truth to hinder us from experiencing the healing power of Christ.

Like Michelle, a dear friend, who is the daughter of a local pastor. Her father was abused and beaten as a child. Because of his deeply wounded spirit, he continued the cycle of abuse towards his own family. He was taught from an early age that the answer to stress and fear was violence. As the family of the pastor, they were at church every time the doors were open. Although her father believed in Jesus, He did not truly follow Him. Michelle was forced to pretend that her family was the ideal, happy family, but behind closed doors, her home was a battlefield.

For years, she endured countless attacks of abuse at the hands of her father. Her father was also unfaithful to her mother, and at age fourteen, she found a letter from her father to her mother where he admitted he was having an affair with her mother's best friend. Her mother's best friend was younger and very pretty, which in Michelle's mind meant that youth and beauty were a requirement for love. Michelle was emotionally broken when she found the letter. She began to feel as though her father represented every man. She developed severe insecurity and for the next several years it led to self-destructive behavior. She spent years dealing with low self-esteem until finally she was shown the love of Christ which opened her heart to the truth of salvation. Michelle's father became King Cruel to Michelle. The cycle was only broken because the light of Christ exposed the sin and unforgiveness of her heart, and Michelle came to know Christ as her personal Savior.

After graduating from high school, God blessed me with a scholarship to Samford University where I attended nursing school. Even as a small girl, I always had a special love for babies. God obviously placed that love in my heart because for the majority of the last 28 years I have been blessed to work as a neonatal nurse. Although I no longer work as a bedside nurse, I am blessed to provide education and family support to families experiencing the NICU journey. I watch daily as the enemy works to convince precious moms that delivering a premature or sick infant was a result of their own inadequacies. Nothing could be further from the truth, but that is Satan's strategy. He plants thoughts of doubt and insecurity into the minds of the most vulnerable.

And then there is the couple struggling with infertility. God's plan is unique and special for every family, but the enemy can take advantage of this situation too. He exploits disappointment in order to create stumbling blocks in the lives of God's children. He never misses an opportunity to instill doubt in a person's mind regarding the faithfulness and goodness of God. Again, these thoughts are lies from the Enemy.

Today, Satan has a new weapon to attack unsuspecting victims. He uses social media to place questionable pictures and words in front of impressionable minds. Images that influence hearts leading them to want more. More beauty, more money, more followers; a mirage that promises satisfaction and happiness but only delivers emptiness. Filtered images of seemingly perfect people are just 'a click' away, in order to suggest that just maybe, you too, can have this life; If only you were just a little bit better or had just a little bit more.

Social media has a place in our world, but it absolutely should have no place in your heart or mine. If used by a person who is secure with their identity found in Christ, social media can be a very positive tool and serve as a platform for good. However, the idol of comparison is dangerous and not to be regarded lightly. If you find yourself feeling down and discouraged after scrolling through your feed, I encourage you to pray. Ask God for wisdom and begin to repeat His truths to your heart and mind. As you grow in your knowledge of who you are in Christ, you will be able to recognize the voice of Satan and filter out the lies of the enemy.

Chapter 4

Her Father's Plan

When Adam and Eve sinned in the garden and hid themselves from God, it led to a broken fellowship with God. He is righteous and Holy and unable to look upon our sin. In the Old Testament, people offered sacrifices to God in order to atone for their sins. The process was complicated and burdensome. Like Jenni, the people had to earn and strive for acceptance. Because of God's rich and merciful love for His children, He made a way for us to receive forgiveness. He sent his perfect son, Jesus, to live on earth as a man and then offered His life as a sacrifice for our sin. He bore the punishment for our sin. When someone asks Jesus to come and dwell in their heart, all of the sin and guilt is wiped away. When God looks upon a follower of Christ, He no longer sees that person, but rather He sees Jesus' perfection. It's the most beautiful exchange imaginable. We exchange our sin for His forgiveness and righteousness. He takes our ashes in exchange for His beauty.

When a person grows up in a destructive home or suffers some sort of injustice at the hands of a person controlled by evil, it requires the truth of God's Word to bring freedom. Circumstances may change quickly, as with Jenni and her ashes, but unless a person truly comes to the saving knowledge of Jesus as their Savior, they never escape the pain and shame of their past. Jenni was removed from her terrible circumstances, but her heart was scarred, and she could not find true freedom until she received forgiveness through Christ -- and then forgave the one who brought her so much pain.

Even after a person receives forgiveness through Christ, Satan continues to work to create doubt. This is why it is so important to read God's Word every single day. In God's infinite wisdom, He knew Satan would not surrender easily. Satan knows ultimately, he has been defeated, but he is determined to interrupt the plan of God. Until Jesus comes back to earth to gather His children once and for all, Satan is relentless in his efforts to undermine God's plan for our lives. Fortunately, God has provided spiritual armor for us to protect against the attacks of Satan. Ephesians 6:11 says, "Put on the full armor of God so that you can take your stand against the devil's schemes."

Satan knows this as well. Part of our spiritual armor includes the truth of God's Word. Satan often provides distractions to prevent us from spending time in the Word. Distractions may include work, busy schedules, social media, financial hardships, sick children, marriage issues, work difficulties, hobbies, and even blessings. That's right, blessings. Satan is a deceiver and he can even trick us into allowing blessings to distract us from spending time with God and from keeping Him first in our lives.

God's Word is designed to align our thoughts with God's will for our lives. It is vital that you and I are intentional in our efforts to spend time getting to know the heart of God. The attributes of God are exactly what a child longs for in the heart of a father, and the bible is God's love letter to His children. In scripture, we learn who God is, and we learn of his heart for us. Psalm 86:15 says, "But you, Lord, are a compassionate and gracious God, slow to anger, abounding in love and faithfulness." Then Romans 5:8 reminds us, 'But God demonstrates his own love for us, in this, while we were still sinners, Christ died for us." God sacrificed his only son to die a cruel death on a cross because of his love for fallible people like you and me. His love is more than enough to set us free. It is God's will for us to be whole and complete in Him so that we may accomplish the plans and purposes He had in mind for us in the beginning of time. Satan knows that the authentic love of God is enough to heal the deepest of wounds, and this is why he works so tirelessly to hinder our time in the Word.

Chapter 5

The Ashes

Jenni's ashes became a symbol of her shame. The King forced her to heap the ash piles right outside the windows of the shack so that it would remind her of who she was and who she would be forever. The King intended for the ashes to extinguish the light of hope from entering the shack, but Satan's intentions were to block all light from entering Jenni's heart. Jesus says, "I am the light of the world" (NIV, John 8:12). Satan knows that once a child of God experiences the light of Christ, his work ends. The King allowed hatred and evil to consume his heart, but even he wasn't aware of Satan's true agenda. Through the actions of the King, Satan planned to wound Jenni's soul deeply in order to create a generational cycle of shame and fear that would never end. His plan was to plant the seed of pride in her heart, so she would harden her heart to the things of God. She would eventually marry and have children, and they too would spend years gathering ashes and placing them around the tiny, broken-down shack. Jenni might have even taught her children how to gather the ashes and spread them so as to not disturb the growing piles; thus ensuring the ever-present darkness of the shack.

Satan will use anyone not focused on serving Christ

to carry out his agenda. Many times, people are unaware that they, like King Cruel, are being used by the enemy. Sin opens the door for Satan to work. Often, it's the little foxes that spoil the vine as spoken about in scripture. It's those "every day" sins like gossip, selfishness, backbiting, jealousy, or greed which Satan uses to introduce sin into our lives.

One of the most destructive weapons of the enemy is an unhappy, discontented heart. A person who lacks the joy of Christ is unable to see clearly. A spirit of 'deserving more' rises up from the seeds planted by Satan and chokes the joy of God from one's life. Toxic, negative thoughts spread to everyone they know. Their judgment of relationships and situations is filtered by pride and rebellion. Satan can create doubt and suspicion against God. A self-focused heart stands in direct opposition to a God-focused heart; producing a heart and mind controlled by the enemy.

Like Jenni, my ashes brought a great deal of insecurity and shame. I learned at an early age that 'pleasing people' led to peace, so that is what I strived to do. I witnessed a lot of unfaithfulness in relationships from the adults in my early life which taught me that value, commitment, and loyalty were all temporary. Vows were broken and love stolen. In my young heart, I internalized the message that the thinner and prettier you are, the more valuable you become. Love was something to be earned and it was something that could be lost.

In Hebrew, the word worship is defined as 'worth-ship'. This means that where you find your value is who or what you are truly worshiping. For years, I found my value in my performance and in the opinions of other people. This means that I made myself and others the objects of my worship. Other people find their value in education, a title, finances, and even in relationships; all of which serve as counterfeits. God alone is worthy of our worship and praise. Our worth and value are found only in Him through our relationship with Jesus Christ. This is why Satan works so hard to assault our minds with thoughts of shame and doubt. He wants us to be distracted from the truth of Salvation so that we continue in the cycle of sin. If he can convince us that our value can be won and lost, then we will stay busy striving and working to earn acceptance from the world. Unfortunately, I fell prey to Satan's deception.

By the time I reached college, I was very vulnerable to the lies of Satan. I ended up in several unhealthy dating relationships until God in his infinite mercy and grace, led me to my precious husband. Unfortunately, the effects of my childhood were far-reaching, and by the time I was engaged, I suffered from undiagnosed anorexia. I weighed ninety pounds on my wedding day, and at 5 feet 4 inches, my secret was exposed.

I carried my shame with such heaviness, there was no room for food in my stomach. I wore it like a heavy jacket; always weighing me down. I remember thinking that somehow, I could control my life by controlling my body. I think subconsciously I restricted my eating and adhered to rigorous exercise as a type of self-punishment. Eating disorders never arise from a place of love, peace, or joy. If you had asked me if I was prideful, I would have likely replied "absolutely not!" After all, I didn't like who I was. How could I possibly have been prideful? As I reflect back on those very difficult days, I now realize that I was incredibly prideful. My attempt to punish myself and my body came from a distorted sense of deserving better; believing that through my sacrifice of food I would attain a better life. Again, Satan used my ashes of shame and self-doubt to cloud my thinking; his plan was working.

From where do your piles of ashes arise? Was it the result of rejection from someone who was supposed to love you? Was it from a dear friend that betrayed you? Maybe it was from the loss of a loved one? Do you feel condemned by your sin? Maybe you feel as though you simply deserve more.

Ashes are defined as 'the remains of something destroyed.' Satan is unrelenting in his effort to hinder the purpose for which God created us. He causes deep, penetrating wounds that cloud our judgment and perception of ourselves, our relationships, and most of all, God. Once he has placed feelings of doubt and unworthiness in our souls, he then interjects counterfeit solutions to our problems. For me, he placed the disease of anorexia in my mind. He whispered deceptive lies into my ears, and because I wasn't aware of who I was in Christ, I fell victim to his lies. For others, he places drugs and alcohol, which desensitize a person to their pain. Clearly, there is always a trap. What a person feels from drug and alcohol abuse soon becomes an insatiable appetite for more and more. The enemy cleverly provides an anesthetic while the abuse ravages the user's body and mind. It is an endless cycle of self-destruction.

Satan also provides counterfeit relationships to fulfill the longings of a wounded soul. It feels like love at the time, but after the damage is done and the compromise is made, Satan pulls away the mask and exposes his true character. The shame and insecurity created by a broken relationship where boundaries were crossed develops wounds that can only be healed by the authentic love of God. Feelings of condemnation and regret flood the mind. Condemnation is not from God, but it is the gateway to shame, and shame is the gateway to sin. The Word says in Romans 8:1, "Therefore, there is now no condemnation for those who are in Christ Jesus, . . ." Satan also knows Scripture and he works overtime to ensure that our guilt and shame keep us on the treadmill of sin.

Jesus waits with open arms to rescue His children. His greatest desire is for us to know Him and the power of His resurrection. Jesus died on the cross and He paid the penalty that we deserve. When you come to Jesus and ask for His forgiveness for your sins, He wipes the sins away. He will never remind you of your sin. If you struggle with feelings of guilt after asking for forgiveness from God, then the voice you hear is not the voice of a loving Father. It is the voice of

Satan; telling you to feel condemned and ashamed.

It's important to realize that once we accept Jesus Christ as Lord and Savior of our lives, we will still be tempted. James 4:7 says, "Submit yourselves, then to God. Resist the devil, and he will flee from you." Close, consistent fellowship with God including studying God's Word is crucial, if we are to stand against the traps of Satan. Ephesians 6:10-17 provides a full battle plan for every believer who is serious about following God's plan and defeating the enemy. It reads, "Finally, be strong in the Lord and in his mighty power. Put on the full armor of God, so that you can take your stand against the devil's schemes, For our struggle is not against flesh and blood, but against the rulers, against the authorities, against the powers of this dark world and against the spiritual forces of evil in the heavenly realms. Therefore put on the full armor of God, so that when the day of evil comes, you may be able to stand your ground, and after you have done everything, to stand. Stand firm then, with the belt of truth buckled around your waist, with the breastplate of righteousness in place, and with your feet fitted with the readiness that comes from the gospel of peace. In addition to all this, take up the shield of faith, with which you can extinguish all the flaming arrows of the evil one. Take the helmet of salvation and the sword of the Spirit, which is the word of God." This paints a picture of a strong and valiant soldier who is resolved in his position, prepared to stand firm in his faith, with the protection of Almighty God.

Chapter 6

The Frozen Smile

By the time I reached adulthood, I struggled with an overwhelming need to earn acceptance and love from others. Just as Jenni, I was afraid of not being who others thought I should be. Satan reminded me daily that I was inferior and like Jenni, I began to believe it. I knew Christ from an early age, and I accepted Him as Savior, but I never truly understood who I was in Christ. I fell prey to an identity defined by the world's perception of me.

I found myself analyzing every conversation and every look; terrified that I would be rejected. I learned to apologize even when something was not my fault, and I learned to smile and agree even when I completely disagreed. I was desperate for approval. My self-worth was determined by the responses and opinions of everyone around me. Satan took full advantage of my vulnerabilities. After all, he was the one who was responsible for the dysfunction I had experienced as a child. Satan knew my weaknesses very well.

Unfortunately, I allowed myself to be in situations that never should have happened. Satan placed a convenient counterfeit in my life at just the right time. He wasn't a bad guy, but like me, he wasn't living the life God intended for him. He was from a Christian family, and he most certainly had many of the qualities I assumed I wanted. He claimed to love me, but that love came with expectations. I was expected to look a certain way, obtain a certain degree, weigh the right amount, and surrender everything I held close to my heart. I felt as though I had to be perfect which led to constant striving and working; never feeling worthy. I found myself deeply conflicted.

Although Satan was the one tempting me to compromise, he was the same one accusing me of my sin. Satan knew I was a believer so he screamed condemnation at me while at the same time reminding me that I would be nothing without the love of a guy. Satan is the cruelest adversary. I wanted to pray and ask the Lord for guidance, but Satan would again remind me of my sin. I felt so unworthy of God's love, I found it difficult to pray. If only I knew of God's heart for me I would have known that He was always there waiting for me; His arms open and ready to forgive me. Despite my distance from Him and the brokenness of my spirit, God had a plan.

Chapter 7

Her Secret Writings

The piles of Jenni's ashes were growing higher by the day, and there was no end in sight to her struggles. She used her finger to write secret letters to God on the wall, begging to be rescued. Like Jenni, I remember my secret letters. As a little girl, I desperately wanted God to reach down and change my family and my life. I know that God heard my prayers. I know that He recorded and saved every tear that I cried. Psalm 56:8 says, "Record my misery; list my tears on your scroll – are they not in your record?" God is compassionate to the lost and hurting. I know that He was with Jenni in the little shack, and He was with me as I wrote secret prayers to Him. God saw my suffering, and He began planning my rescue as He did for Jenni. And friend, He will do the same for you. Often, His timeline is different from ours, but He hears every prayer, and He will always answer on time.

Jenni and I knew at a young age that our ashes were placed upon us by Satan. We wrote secret letters, and God answered us with perfect timing. It is actually difficult to imagine growing up in a dysfunctional environment and not being aware of the enemy's influence. Sadly, this is something that happens to God's children every day.

Charlotte, a nurse for many years, is funny, kind, and loving. She never meets a stranger, and she makes you feel as though you have known her for years, despite having just met her. She is one of those precious jewels who radiates joy. When I met Charlotte, we were working on a project together, and our personalities just clicked. As I got to know Charlotte, I began to see clues of insecurity. One night over dinner, she opened up about her struggles spiritually and her difficult childhood. She shared that her mother had been abused by her stepfather and that Charlotte was conceived as a result of the abuse. Before the age of twelve, Charlotte had also suffered abuse by several older family members. She grew up without a father until her mother married a man named Mike. Mike was a counterfeit and he only added to Charlotte's ever-growing pile of ashes. At the time, Charlotte was unaware that the things done to her were abusive. Satan's intention was to wound her spirit deeply in the shadow of darkness.

A shadow is defined as 'a dark area produced when rays of light are blocked' and also as 'ominous, oppressiveness or sadness and gloom'. Satan's plan was for Charlotte to remain in the darkness, but God saw her shame and was preparing her escape! In John 9, Jesus was walking along when He came upon a man who was born blind. Jesus opened the man's eyes and gave him sight. Until Jesus touched his eyes, he could not see the light of Christ. Once the darkness is exposed to light, the counterfeit is revealed.

Charlotte shared that she was invited to attend church with a friend and accepted Christ as a thirteen-year-old girl. Just like the blind man, she remained in darkness until Jesus Christ opened her eyes. His light exposed the abuse that had been committed in secret, and Christ began to heal her wounded soul. Charlotte was born into dysfunction and suffered through no fault of her own. God saw every injustice and every tear she cried.

Following our dinner together, we sat in my car, and Charlotte recommitted her life to Christ. To this day, she continues to seek Him through reading His Word, and He faithfully reveals Himself to her. She is learning to walk in freedom and joy, as daily, God is casting her ashes to the wind. No tear was unnoticed, and no pain suffered in vain. For God promises in Psalm 126:5, "Those who sow with tears will reap with songs of joy." Charlotte is not a result of her stepfather's sin. She is a beautiful reminder of the grace and mercy of God. She is discovering her identity as a child of the Most High God, and she has traded her ashes for His crown of beauty.

Chapter 8

And Then Suddenly

Jenni spent years gathering ashes. The piles were enormous, and the buckets she used to collect the ashes were small. She emptied thousands upon thousands of buckets in her early years. The days of struggle seemed as though they would never end.

In my own life, I can remember being fourteen-years-old and wondering if I would make it to age eighteen. When you are in the midst of a trial, it's often difficult to know when it will end. There are many times in life when we pray for answers to problems, and it seems like God isn't listening or that He isn't concerned. The truth of the matter is that God is working on our behalf even when it seems like He is silent. I can remember begging God to change my situation as a young girl, only to wake the next morning and discover the problem was still there. I realize now that God was working. He had already provided His Son for me, and He was preparing my future husband. He was lining up my scholarship to Samford University, and He was preparing the way for the birth of my precious daughters. He was working in the heart of Joyce Meyer as He led her to write the books that a dear friend would one day share with me. I couldn't see Him working, but He was there all the time; working out every detail of my escape and preparing His best for me.

He is doing the same for you. Just when it seems that nothing will ever change, God is planning your answer, a way for your future, a healing for your heart. Just as in the story with Jenni and the king, God is preparing your escape. Jenni spent years living under the burden of the decree, and she felt as if nothing would ever change. Although the king appeared to Jenni as a force that would last forever; suddenly, in a matter of seconds, he was gone.

Chapter 9

Letting Go of the Ashes

My first job as a NICU nurse was in a small unit in Birmingham. I was blessed to work alongside a precious charge nurse who seemed to take on the role of a 'mother figure' in our unit. Sadly, we lost one of the precious preemies in our unit, and because I had developed an attachment to the family, I felt compelled to attend the funeral to offer my support. My charge nurse asked me to attend church with her and her husband the same day as the funeral. The location of the funeral home was close to their church, so I could attend the funeral with her following the church service that morning.

At her church, on that fateful Sunday morning, I met the man that I would forever compare every other man against. Alex was handsome and incredibly kind. As he spoke about Christ during the Sunday school class that day, I knew something was different about him. To my surprise, he called me the next week and we began dating. As our relationship progressed, I began to realize that he was unlike any man I had ever dated. He treated me with such kindness, he followed through on what he said he would do, and he showed respect toward me and to everyone. He appeared to be a man of true integrity. Most importantly, Alex had always held true to his convictions; sadly I could not say the same. I felt unworthy of Alex, so I began planning his exit.

I felt the guilt of decisions I had made years before. I compromised my values in order to be loved and accepted by a guy who eventually proved to be a counterfeit. He was strategically placed in my life by the enemy. Because I was wearing my 'pleasing smile' and had ashes in my eyes, I didn't recognize the danger until it was too late.

Through dating Alex, a true Christ-follower, I became much more aware of my sin. I planned to confess it all to Alex and then break up with him. I thought this would make everything easier in the long run. I arranged to drive to Nashville one night to talk with a friend from college about the best way to deliver the news to Alex. My friend and her new husband were Christians. They prayed with me and encouraged me to pray on the way home before talking with Alex.

The next weekend was Valentine's weekend. Alex had already planned a date for us. How ironic that I was thinking of ending our relationship on Valentine's weekend. On Friday night, I told Alex everything. . . and I mean everything. He sat there quietly, holding my hand. His first comment to me was that we have all sinned. He then went on to say that I didn't need to ask for his forgiveness. He shared his faith with me and extended more grace to me than I had ever received from any other person. I could not comprehend how this precious, wonderful man could possibly look at me the same way, but he did.

Alex asked me out for the next night, so I reluctantly assumed he was willing to continue dating me.

On Saturday night, Alex picked me up for our date and we drove to a local restaurant for dinner. At the end of the date, we returned to his home. Alex said he had something to discuss with me. I thought to myself, "This is it. He has had time to think about it, and now he is going to end it." I remember not feeling surprised and almost relieved; after all, I was not worthy of him, and now I could stop pretending that I was.

He sat down and looked at me, picked up his Bible and began reading. He read Genesis 2:24 which says, "That is why a man leaves his father and mother and is united to his wife, and they become one flesh." He read several other scriptures, and then he got down on one knee, told me for the first time that he loved me, and asked me to marry him!

He began to share with me that while I was in Nashville, he was at the home of my grandparents, asking for my hand in marriage. While Satan was convincing me that I was unworthy of Alex, the Lord was leading him to ask for my hand in marriage! I was overwhelmed by the love and grace of God. The Lord saw me through all of those years of shame and sadness, and He was planning my escape. He knew my prince would come, and He answered every single prayer beautifully and in His perfect time.

Dear Friend, He sees you right now at this very moment! I am praying for you as I type these words. Like Jenni, who lived in 'The Kingdom of Not So Far Away', you are never so far away that God cannot reach you. You have always been in His loving embrace. Even when you can't see or feel Him, He is there; planning and preparing a way for you. I pray that no matter where you are or what you are going through, you will know deep within your heart that God loves you right now. He loved you yesterday, He loves you today, and He will love you tomorrow! Like Jenni and me, your Father loves you and He is in control of your future. He is planning your escape.

I eventually married my precious Alex. He represented the opposite of everything I had experienced as a child. He knew the Lord and he loved me because of His love and devotion to Christ. I believe that is something missing in the teaching for so many young women today. We are lied to by the world and told that we must weigh a certain amount or look a certain way, that we must have this or that degree, or present the perfect image; then and only then will we be worthy of the love of a good man. This is a deception from Satan. Only true and authentic love from Christ can sustain a marriage or relationship. My husband loves me because of His love and devotion to Christ. If my behavior or appearance were responsible for keeping my husband devoted to me, he would have stopped loving me a long time ago.

I would love to tell you that my life became a fairy tale, but that would be a lie. Our first year of marriage was especially difficult. Due to my insecurity, I became terribly anxious each morning when Alex left for work. I worried incessantly that he would change his mind about loving me and not return home. My thoughts were completely irrational. After all, his clothes were there! But I was so wounded. The eyes of my heart were trying to view love through my ashes of shame. I didn't have a true understanding of love; especially the love of our Creator.

I am beyond thankful that Alex's love and marriage vows were a commitment to God and not just to me. This is why it is so important not to date someone who only claims to be a Christian, but to pray and ask God for wisdom to choose a true Christ-follower. Being a believer is important but being a follower of Christ is what God wants for you. The world is filled with people who claim to believe in God, but until they experience a true relationship with God through Christ, they cannot know the abundant life Jesus promises them.

For me, the revelation of who I was in Christ came in 2005. By this time, I had three precious daughters and I had been married to my sweet Alex for several years. We built a home and a beautiful life together. I should have been joyful and secure, but I was not. I doubted my abilities as a mom and as a wife. I questioned my purpose, my value, and my life. I accepted Christ into my heart as a seven-year-old, but I could not understand why I lacked security and joy. I was discontent and found myself fearful and worrying constantly as I had as a child. I was blessed with a beautiful life, but it was as if someone had put blinders on my eyes. I could not see it. All I could see was the reflection of myself as a little girl. I wasn't enough and I would never be enough. I was carrying a burden of guilt and shame. I also struggled with resentment toward the adults in my childhood who I felt were responsible for my wounds.

Like Jenni from the story, I could not see myself as Christ saw me. I found myself constantly comparing my life, my weight, my home, my abilities, and even my purpose to those around me. I felt hopeless. Satan used my shame to drive me even further into darkness. In my desperation, I reached out to a dear friend for help. I called her and she agreed to meet me. She gave me several books from a teacher that God had used in her own life that led to her healing. That night I read fervently through the pages of Joyce Meyer's books, *Battlefield of the Mind* and *Approval Addiction*. All I can say is that I felt the Lord anointed the words on those pages just for me. All the years of pain and shame surfaced, and the Lord used Joyce's books along with the Word of God to bring true healing to my heart. I began crying and I don't think I stopped crying for several days. God did a work in my heart that can only be described as miraculous. I wondered how I could have been in church my entire life and missed the message that God loved me and gave His son in exchange for my brokenness and sin. He took my guilt and pain and gave me His love and forgiveness. I had been trying to earn something for years that I already possessed!

The Truth pierced my heart that night and I've never been the same. I realized that Satan had a plan to destroy my family and it was a plan that was generations in the making. Even though I grew up in dysfunction, God loved me and provided an escape from my past. The most beautiful part was that He was always there. Even when I was in the darkness, He was right there waiting for me to call His name. He knew about my precious Alex and the three precious daughters that He would one day bring into my life. When I look back, I am overwhelmed with gratitude from God's love and provision for my life. I made so many mistakes prior to meeting my husband, but God in His infinite wisdom sees where we are, and has a plan for us. He understands the 'why' behind our decisions. His love and compassion are all-encompassing.

The day I realized my value in Christ is the day I truly began to live the abundant life God planned for me. I began seeking Christ like never before. I craved time with Him. I knew in order to grow in my walk with Christ that I needed more teaching and a desire grew in my heart to seek Him like never before. The Word tells us in Jeremiah 29:13, "You will seek me and find me when you seek me with all your heart." He never lies and He never breaks His promises. Over the next several years, God provided wonderful evangelists, teachers, and authors to speak His truth into my heart. I began a new journey of discovering all that God had for my life. God healed my heart and my mind; a heart that should have required intensive counseling.

Jesus is more than enough for you too. His love is not dependent on what you do or who you are – His love is unconditional and undying. His love is perfect and eternal. He loves you at your best and He loves you at your worst. He loves you before your sin and He loves you after your sin. My prayer for you is that you would know the love shared in Ephesians 3:17(b)-18, "And I pray that you, being rooted and established in love, may have power, together with all of the Lord's holy people, to grasp how wide and long and high and deep is the love of Christ . . . "

In scripture He is the Almighty One, the Alpha and Omega, our Advocate, the Author and Perfecter of our Faith, He is our Authority, the Bread of Life, Beloved Son of God, The Bridegroom, The Chief Cornerstone, Our Deliverer, The Faithful and True One, The Good Shepherd, Immanuel, The Holy Servant, The King of Kings, The Lamb of God, The Light of the World, The Messiah, The Mediator, The One Who Sets Free, Our Peace, Our Hope, Our Redeemer . . . the list goes on and on. He loves you, and He desires to meet every need in your life. You only need to surrender to Him.

Romans 10:9-10 says, "If you declare with your mouth, 'Jesus Is Lord,' and believe in your heart that God raised him from the dead, you will be saved. For it is with your heart that you believe and are justified, and it is with your mouth that you profess your faith and are saved." If you are new in your faith or maybe you are like me; a follower of Christ for years who is ready to experience Christ in a deeper and more personal way, please reach out to me or some other trusted Christian friend. I would love to celebrate your decision and to encourage you on your journey. God knows your heart and He knows where you are right now. I am praying that you will begin reading His Word, and you will know His love for you as it becomes imprinted upon your heart.

Chapter 10

Your Crown of Beauty

To replace your ashes for His crown of beauty, you must study and learn God's Word. As I began seeking Christ and reading my Bible, not only did I learn who Christ is, I also began to learn who I am (in Christ). I began to understand the worth and value that God placed on me from the very beginning of my life. Because Satan spends a lifetime attacking you through your thoughts, it's important to fill your mind and heart with what God says about you. Although salvation happens immediately when you receive Christ as your Lord and Savior, it requires time reading God's Word and time in prayer to understand His plan for you. Below is a list of scriptures that reveal who you are in Christ. Whenever Satan tries to hinder your growth in Christ, use scripture to talk back to him just as Jesus did. Soon you will no longer have to read the verses; the more you repeat them, the more they will be brought to your memory (through the Holy Spirit). As you repeat the confessions that follow and read each verse, I encourage you to pray and ask the Lord to manifest His love and plan for your life.

•Because of my faith in Christ, I am brand new. My old way of thinking and living is gone. I am free to live as my Father intends; joyfully and with thankfulness.

"Therefore, if anyone is in Christ, the new creation has come: The old has gone, the new is here!" (NIV, 2 Corinthians 5:17)

•I was created for a purpose by Almighty God.

"For we are God's handiwork, created in Christ Jesus to do good works, which God prepared in advance for us to do." (NIV, Ephesians 2:10)

•Condemnation is not from God. As His child, when He looks at me, He sees only Jesus.

"Therefore, there is now no condemnation for those who are in Christ Jesus, . . ." (NIV, Romans 8:1)

•Christ is alive in me.

"I have been crucified with Christ and no longer live, but Christ lives in me. The life I now live in the body, I live by faith in the Son of God, who loved me and gave himself for me." (NIV, Galatians 2:20)

•God lives in me through the Holy Spirit and He has overcome the enemy!

"You, dear children, are from God and have overcome them, because the one who is in you is greater than the one who is in the world." (NIV, 1 John: 4:4)

•I am one with Christ!

"But whoever is united with the Lord is one with him in spirit." (NIV, 1 Corinthians 6:17)

•I have been made right with God through my acceptance of Jesus as my Lord and Savior. He loves me and He is pleased with me.

"Therefore, since we have been justified by faith, we have peace with God through our Lord Jesus Christ, . . ." (NIV, Romans 5:1)

•Christ chose me to represent Him in my life. I will do good works because of His love for me and my love for Him. I desire to spread the Gospel in His name. He is my good, and perfect Father, who desires to answer when I call upon His name.

"You did not choose me, but I chose you and appointed you so that you might go and bear fruit – fruit that will last – so that whatever you ask in my name, the Father will give you." (NIV, John 15:16)

•Nothing can separate me from God's love.

"No, in all these things we are more than conquerors through him who loved us." (NIV, Romans 8:37)

•I am an awe-inspiring creation of my Father. I am fully convinced of His love for me. Any good in my life is because of His character and heart for me.

"I praise you, for I am fearfully and wonderfully made; your works are wonderful, I know that full well." (NIV, Psalm 139:14)

•The light of Christ guides me to truth and His light shines through me and leads others to Him.

"You are the light of the world. A town built on a hill cannot be hidden." (NIV, Matthew 5:14)

•Christ lives in me; therefore, I can approach God with boldness with faith that He is my Father and cares deeply for me.

"In him and through faith in him we may approach God with freedom and confidence." (NIV, Ephesians 3:12)

•God is my rescuer and He has brought me out of darkness and into His beautiful light. I belong to my Father and because I belong to Him, He is merciful to me.

"But you are a chosen people, a royal priesthood, a holy nation, God's special possession, that you may declare the praises of him who called you out of darkness into his wonderful light. Once you were not a people, but now you are the people of God; once you had not received mercy, but now you have received mercy." (NIV, 1 Peter 2:9-10)

•God has broken Satan's grip on me, and I am now a part of God's family through Christ Jesus.

"For he has rescued us from the dominion of darkness and brought us into the kingdom of the Son he loves, . . ." (NIV, Colossians 1:13)

•God has saved me by His grace, and He will continue to change me day by day as I learn more and more of His heart.

". . . being confident of this, that he who began a good work in you will carry it on to completion until the day of Christ Jesus." (NIV, Philippians 1:6)

•Jesus died on the cross and paid the penalty for my sin. I have been made right with God through my acceptance of His sacrifice.

". . . and all are justified freely by his grace through the redemption that came by Christ Jesus." (NIV, Romans 3:24)

•I will not be anxious or fearful of anything because I will pray and share my concerns with God. I will praise Him at all times and thank Him for all that He has done in my life and I will enjoy the peace which God has provided for me.

"Do not be anxious about anything, but in every situation, by prayer and petition, with thanksgiving, present your requests to God. And the peace of God, which transcends all understanding, will guard your hearts and your minds in Christ Jesus." (NIV, Philippians 4:6-7)

•Jesus suffered and died for my sins. By His sacrifice I am completely healed.

"But he was pierced for our transgressions, he was crushed for our iniquities; the punishment that brought us peace was on him, and by his wounds we are healed." (NIV, Isaiah 53:5)

Chapter 11

The New Reflection

As you begin to discover who you are in Christ, you will begin to see yourself in the light of Christ. Just as Jenni, you can remove your tattered clothes of despair and exchange them for beautiful garments of praise. When Satan sends thoughts of worry or fear, you can talk back to the enemy using the Word of God. You are the loved, highly esteemed child of the Creator, and He is pleased with you right now. When He looks at you, He sees Jesus. Jesus is in you in the form of the sweet Holy Spirit. He will never leave you. His love will heal your wounded heart. The thoughts of shame and fear once a part of your life will disappear. When you walk through difficulties or problems, you will no longer feel unloved or insecure. Rather, you will be at peace knowing that you are no longer tormented by the enemy, but now you have the mind of Christ.

Psalm 34:8 says, "Taste and see that the Lord is good; blessed is the one who takes refuge in him." There are a lot of things in life that you can experience second hand, but friend, God is not one of them. You can learn about Him and his goodness, but to truly experience God, you must be in need of trusting Him. As you allow yourself to deal with areas of weakness and pain, you find that your own reflection becomes filtered through God's view of you. As you lean into His love and see yourself as He sees you, your view of yourself will change. You will begin to recognize His hand all throughout your life as He was carefully lining up every detail for your rescue. He has been pursuing you all of your life; even when you were collecting your ashes. God has carefully taken into consideration all of your scars and imperfections and He plans to use them for His glory! 2 Corinthians 12:9 says, "My grace is sufficient for you, for my power is made perfect in weakness." Therefore I will boast all the more gladly about my weaknesses, so that Christ's power may rest on me."

Seeing your reflection through the filter of God's eyes is a daily choice. The enemy may still tempt you to pick up your tattered clothes of despair, but you know who you are and you know "whose" you are! Satan no longer has any authority over you, because you belong to the One who died and gave himself in exchange for your life. When you are tempted to pick up your ashes, remind yourself of God's truth. Rehearse the promises he provides in His word, play your favorite praise music, and thank the Father that you are loved, forgiven, and chosen! Friend, as you grow in your knowledge of His heart and character, your reflection will return to you as a testimony of his strength and love; His faithfulness on display for all the world to see!

Chapter 12

The Display of His Glory

At the beginning of this book, I shared Isaiah 61. I would love for you to read it again at the end of the book in light of who you are in Christ. The chapter speaks to the fact that we are healed and forgiven in order to serve God and spread the Gospel. If you have received Christ as your Lord and Savior, you are free of the shame of your past. Or you may be like me – I was a believer for years, but I didn't fully understand who I was in Christ. I am so thankful that you now see Truth and that Satan no longer has authority over your life. You can walk in the light of Christ and experience the joy and the abundant life He's provided for you.

Dear friend, your story and your pain are not in vain. God will take what Satan intends for harm and use it for His glory. Your story may one day be what God uses to lead a friend out of their darkness and into the light of Truth.

You are loved, forgiven, treasured, adored, and redeemed! As a follower of Christ, your old life has passed away and your new life has begun. Just like the tiny broken shack, you are no longer hidden by piles of soaring ashes. Instead, you live among the lovely colored flowers and soar alongside oaks of righteousness; you are a planting of the Lord. You exemplify the Father's splendor and glory and remind others of His love for you who know your story.

Chapter 13

From Castle Life to Kingdom Living

We end this story with Jenni discovering her worth and value in Christ. Just like me, she is no longer a prisoner of Satan's lies and deceit. She has accepted Christ as her Lord and Savior and has begun her journey of healing and restoration. The ashes have vanished, the king no longer has her in his grasp, and she is free to be all her Heavenly Father wants her to be. She is learning to find her worth and value in Christ. She acknowledges her full dependence on God. But what now? What is God's intent for His children and why is it so important that believers learn to be led by the Holy Spirit?

Christ's command for His followers is to share the Gospel. We should seek Him above everything else, and He will provide what we need, when we need it. As we allow God to change our hearts and heal our wounds, His will for our lives will become clearer. Our main focus should be to chase after Christ and to practice kingdom living. Matthew 6:33 says, "But seek first his kingdom and his righteousness, and all these things will be given to you as well." Kingdom living means that we should live our lives obedient to God's commands and share the Gospel throughout the world. We are no longer slaves to the sins of the world. By the power of God at work in us through the

Holy Spirit, we are to fulfill the Great Commission thereby fulfilling God's plan for our lives. The Great Commission is spoken about by Jesus in Matthew 28:18-20. He said, "All authority in heaven and on earth has been given to me. Therefore go and make disciples of all nations, baptizing them in the name of the Father and of the Son and of the Holy Spirit, and teaching them to obey everything I have commanded you. And surely I am with you always, to the very end of the age."

God's original intention was for man to rule over His creation; but after the fall of man in the garden; that all changed (Genesis 3). We became preoccupied with ourselves and our desires rather than seeking God's ways. God sent Jesus to restore the original order and to provide a way (through salvation) for man to become part of His Kingdom. Matthew 4:17 says, "From that time on Jesus began to preach, 'Repent, for the kingdom of heaven has come near.'" God, out of His abundant love for man, provides a way for us to enjoy complete freedom through Christ while sharing His gospel to the lost world.

It would not be enough for Jenni to simply live happily ever after in the castle. She must recognize that sharing the love of Christ with others in 'The Land of Not So Far Away' is paramount in fulfilling God's plan for her life. It is not enough that when she looks into the mirror, she sees a new reflection; she must "proclaim the kingdom of God and teach about the Lord Jesus — with all boldness and without hindrance!" with emphasis from Acts 28:31. Christ rescued us! What Satan means for harm; God uses for His glory.

It will be important for Jenni to put God first in her life. Jenni's value now is found in her relationship with Christ and her joy is found in her service to God. In Luke 4:8, Jesus answered, "It is written: Worship the Lord your God and serve him only." It is also important that Jenni remains obedient to God. There are guidelines for behavior that God provides in His word to help us remain in His will, but He may also require more from you than you feel qualified or prepared to accomplish.

When our daughters were ages seven, five, and two, I felt the Lord calling me to homeschool them. My two oldest daughters were attending a public elementary school that was filled with Christian teachers and wonderful, Godly families. I could not understand why God would ask me to leave such a wonderful environment. I was on the PTO board and a room mother for both daughters' classes. My oldest daughter was blessed with two Christian teachers; 5 children in her class prayed to receive Christ with the teachers earlier in the school year! I wrestled with the decision and thought of countless excuses for why homeschooling was not for us. I tried to tell myself I was being too spiritual, and that God wasn't seriously asking me to do something that seemed so radical.

One Sunday, as I was getting ready for church, I heard "In Touch Ministries" on the television. Charles Stanley was preaching and as I rounded the corner to our den, I heard him share one of his life principles. He stated, "Obey God and leave all of the consequences to Him." I knew in an instant that God was speaking directly to me. I was terrified, but obedient.

When I look back, I'm overwhelmed by God's provision and faithfulness. When we obey God and leave the consequences to Him; He honors our obedience. There is a great deal of freedom that comes when we relinquish control to the Lord. Trusting the Lord with our girls didn't ensure problem-free lives, but I know that no matter what comes, the Lord will be faithful to His promises. Despite my doubts and weaknesses, He remained faithful. Without His guidance, we would not be where we are today. The decision to homeschool nor our parenting led to the blessings we received. They were the result of prayer and obedience to God. He is faithful to lead, and we must be faithful to obey. I am not sure what God's plan for each of their lives will look like, but I know I can trust Him with their futures. I am so thankful that I have learned that his faithfulness is based on who He is and not on who we are!

We began homeschooling our oldest daughter when she was in the third grade; she is now a senior at Samford University. Our middle daughter is in nursing school at Lee University, and our youngest is a senior in high school and will be attending The University of Alabama this fall. There were many days when I struggled with insecurity related to my abilities to teach them, but God always provided exactly what we needed. Our daughters are not perfect, but they are kind and loving and share a deep love for Christ. Like me, they must walk their own journey in discovering their worth and value in the Lord. They will have good days and some bad days, and through both they will learn to experience God first hand. As they grow in their relationships with Him, we pray that their love for the Gospel continues to grow. Alex and I gave our girls to the Lord a long time ago, and we are trusting Him to accomplish His plans and purposes through their lives.

God's plan for your family and your life may look completely different, but friend, the beauty of God's plan is that it is for you; designed specifically for you! His goal for all of us is to share the Gospel with the world, but He uses us all in different ways to accomplish that assignment.

We've shared a lot together throughout the last several chapters. I want to review Romans 12:1-2: "Therefore, I urge you, brothers and sisters, in view of God's mercy, to offer your bodies as a living sacrifice, holy and pleasing to God – this is your true and proper worship. Do not conform to the pattern of this world but be transformed by the renewing of your mind. Then you will be able to test and approve what God's will is – his good, pleasing, and perfect will." Paul is speaking to believers in this passage. He stresses the importance of being set apart from the world. God desires our obedience inwardly, as well as our outward obedience. He is asking for a commitment of our love and devotion to Him. He calls us 'living sacrifices' because He desires selfless lives of service to Him. The animal sacrifices in the old testament were dead, but we present ourselves as living sacrifices by the dedication of our lives to Christ. It's Christ in us and the new life He provides for us that makes this possible. We are encouraged to 'renew our minds' so that we will be able to comprehend God's will. We do this by reading and studying God's Word. Just as with Jenni, the ashes from her past were removed, but it required the revelation of God's Word to change her thinking and her heart.

Jenni's story ends with her newfound security in Christ and all appears to be well; a real fairytale ending. Life, however, is not a fairytale. When we become followers of Christ, we are not guaranteed problem-free lives. In John 16:33, Jesus says, "I have told you these things, so that in me you may have peace. In this world, you will have trouble. But take heart! I have overcome the world." We live in a fallen world where sin is prevalent, but Jesus promises that He has won the victory! As followers of Christ, we have confidence in His love and provision. While we seek God and love others, God provides grace to help us endure hardships or problems. Remember God is sovereign, and His timing and plans are perfect.

God blessed me with a wonderful friend named Kate. Kate has a beautiful spirit and reflects the light of Christ to everyone she meets. She grew up in a Christ-centered home. Her dad was a pastor and her mother was loving and Godly. She had an older sister, beautiful and kind, and an older brother, who made even the most serious person burst from laughter.

Her brother, Shane, was a popular seventeen-year-old. He was a talented musician and his personality and laughter were contagious. Growing up in the South, Shane was like most Southern boys; he loved to hunt. On his best friend's birthday, the two boys decided to go hunting in the woods behind Shane's home. He and his friend were hunting – all safety concerns in check – when suddenly a shot rang out; the shot was not from either of the boys' guns. There was a trespassing hunter in the woods that day, and he accidentally shot Shane; the hunter saw movement in the woods and fired before realizing it was a teenage boy. Upon hearing the terrifying shouts of the hunter, Kate's mom ran to find Shane, alive, but gravely injured. Shane took his last breath in his mothers' arms that day. Kate, who was only fifteen-years-old at the time, and her dad, rushed to the hospital to find Shane lifeless. She recalls how she and her father prayed over Shane and pleaded with the Lord to bring him back to life. God did not revive her brother that day, but he was welcomed into Heaven.

Kate recounts how she woke up early the next morning to a "suffocating grief". She shared that even in those difficult moments, the Lord was there. The day after the shooting, the hunter knocked on their door. He was there to ask for forgiveness. The most beautiful part of this story is that my friend's parents, despite their own grief and heartache, shared the Gospel with the hunter that day and prayed with him to receive Christ. What a beautiful expression of the love of Christ and the fulfillment of the Gospel. Through the power of the Holy Spirit in them, sharing the love of Christ and the truth of salvation became more important than their own pain. We, like the hunter, deserve punishment, but like Kate's parents, God has extended to us great mercy. He allowed his son to die an undeserved death so that we might have eternal life.

God gave the Holy Spirit to dwell in the hearts of those who have accepted Him as Savior. He is faithful to sustain us through even the most difficult circumstances so that He might be glorified. He promises to exchange our despair and brokenness for His joy and praise. He provides for those who walk in obedience to Him, and He rebukes those who inflict pain and suffering upon His children. He takes our former shame and replaces it with a double portion of blessing and everlasting joy. Through our relationship with Jesus Christ, we are called oaks of righteousness as we are rooted in Him, and we will eternally rejoice in the light of His glory.

As you surrender to the Lord, He will take what Satan intended for your harm and use it to bring glory to His name. Just as the soil causes the seed to sprout and the garden to grow, our Sovereign Lord will heal your heart and lead you to share the Gospel. And for this reason alone, my precious friend, you are more than enough.

Isaiah 61

The Spirit of the Sovereign Lord is on me,
because the Lord has anointed me
to proclaim good news to the poor.
He has sent me to bind up the brokenhearted,
to proclaim freedom for the captives
and release from darkness for the prisoners,
to proclaim the year of the Lord's favor
and the day of vengeance of our God,
to comfort all who mourn,
and provide for those who grieve in Zion—
to bestow on them a crown of beauty
instead of ashes,
the oil of joy
instead of mourning,
and a garment of praise
instead of a spirit of despair.
They will be called oaks of righteousness,
a planting of the Lord
for the display of his splendor.

They will rebuild the ancient ruins
and restore the places long devastated;
they will renew the ruined cities
that have been devastated for generations.
Strangers will shepherd your flocks;
foreigners will work your fields and vineyards.
And you will be called priests of the Lord,
you will be named ministers of our God.
Your will feed on the wealth of nations,
and in their riches, you will boast.

Instead of your shame
you will receive a double portion,
and instead of disgrace
you will rejoice in your inheritance.
And so, you will inherit a double
portion in your land,
and everlasting joy will be yours.

For I, the Lord, love justice;
I hate robbery and wrongdoing.
In my faithfulness, I will reward my people
and make an everlasting covenant with them.
Their descendants will be known among the nations
and their offspring among the peoples.
All who see them will acknowledge
that they are a people the Lord has blessed.

I delight greatly in the Lord;
my soul rejoices in my God.
For he has clothed me with garments of salvation
and arrayed me in a robe of his righteousness,
as a bridegroom adorns his head like a priest,
and as a bride adorns herself with her jewels.
For as the soil makes the sprout come up
and a garden causes seeds to grow,
so, the Sovereign Lord will make righteousness
and praise spring up before all nations.

I WAS BROKEN.

NOW I'M HEALED.

JESUS MADE ALL THE
DIFFERENCE.